# Contents / Inhalt

## Pronunciation / Aussprache

| | |
|---|---|
| ee | as in b**ee**, s**ee** |
| i | as in **i**t, w**i**sh |
| eh | as in égalit**é** (franz.), **e**del (dt.) |
| ey,ay | as in th**ey**, d**ay** |
| e | as in **a**go, **a**rrival |
| ah | as in f**a**ther, **a**rm |
| a | as in b**u**t, m**u**ch |
| aw | as in l**aw**, **a**ll |
| ow | as in c**ow**, h**ow** |
| oh | as in plat**eau** (franz.), **o**ben (dt.) |
| o | as in n**o**, s**o** |
| op/om | as in l**o**t, n**o**t |
| oo (doo) | as in t**oo**, y**ou** |
| ch | as in mu**ch**, cat**ch** *(without abdominal breath / ohne Zwerchfell)* |
| ts | as in ca**ts** *(without abdominal breath / ohne Zwerchfell)* |

Bertrand Gröger

# Loop Songs

44 Warm-Up and Performance Studies
for Jazz, Pop and Gospel Choirs

SATB a cappella, optional p (b, dr) | Jazz, Pop, Gospel
Difficulty: 2-5 | Duration: 2.5 h

**ED 20368-01**
ISMN 979-0-001-15826-8

## Singer's Edition
## Ausgabe für Chorsänger

Mainz · London · Berlin · Madrid · New York · Paris · Prague · Tokyo · Toronto
© 2009 Schott Music GmbH & Co. KG, Mainz · Printed in Germany

1. Auflage 5 4 3 2 1 /2012/11 10 09

Alle Drucke dieser Auflage sind unverändert und können im Unterricht nebeneinander
benutzt werden. Die letzte Zahl bezeichnet das Jahr des Drucks.

Umschlaggestaltung: Wega-Verlag GmbH, Mainz
Notensatz und Layout: Klaus Frech

# African Call

Bertrand Gröger

52 813

# Afro-Hey

Bertrand Gröger

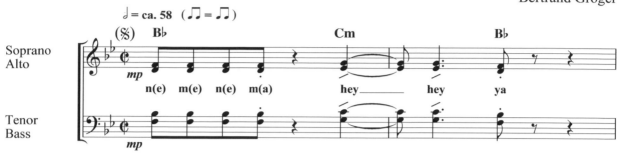

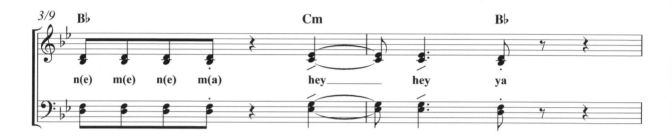

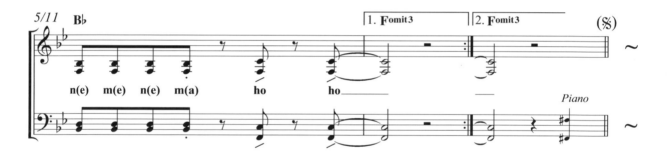

OPTION:  Hand Claps

# Anthem to Hymn

Bertrand Gröger

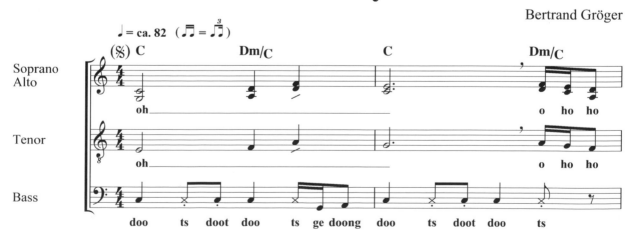

OPTION: **Hand Claps**

# Basses First

Bertrand Gröger

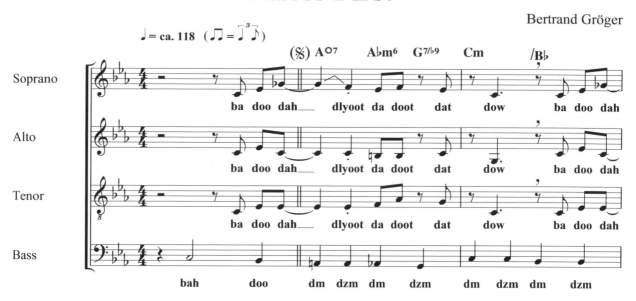

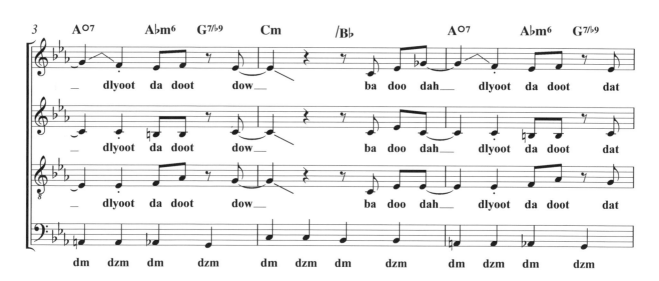

52 813

# Be Concise!

Bertrand Gröger

♩ = ca. 136  (♫ = ♫)

**Soprano Alto**

(%) D    /C    G⁷/B    B♭⁷    Aˢᵘˢ    A⁷    D    (%)

da be doo dat   dat   dow___   dat dat   da be doo dat   dat   dow___

**Tenor Bass**

OPTION:  **Switch the groove...**  Switch to Swing feel (♫ = ♪³♪) and back to straight 8th (on cue)

# Blurred

Bertrand Gröger

♩ = ca. 90  (♫ = ♫)

**Soprano**

(%) $p$ Emᵃᵈᵈ⁹    ∕.    Cᵃᵈᵈ⁹

doo   doo___   doo_____ doo   doo doo   doo   doo___   doo___

**Alto**

$p$

doo doo  doo doo   doo  doo___   doo doo   doo doo doo   doo doo   doo doo   doo doo

**Tenor**

$p$

doo___ doo   doo   doo___   doo doo   doo___ doo

**Bass**

$p$

doo_____   doot  doo_____

**4**  ∕.

Amᵃᵈᵈ⁹    ∕.

doo   doo doo   doo   doo___   doo   doo   doo

$p$

doo doo   doo doo doo   doo doo   doo doo   doo doo___   doo doo   doo doo   doot

$p$

doo   doo___   doo doo   doo___   doo   doo   doo___   doo

doot  doo_____   doot

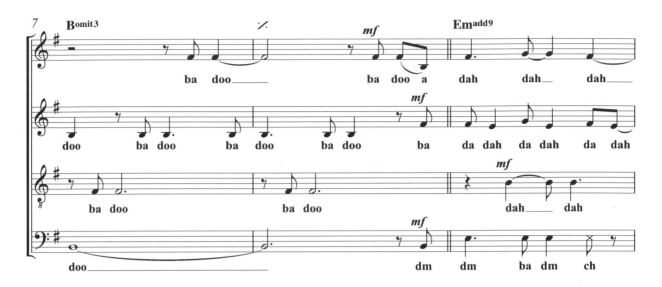

# Brownie

Bertrand Gröger

# Chach

Bertrand Gröger

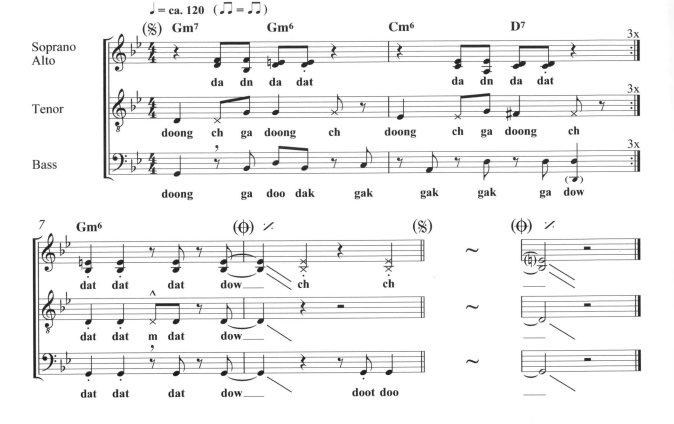

# Chorale (From Dawn to Dusk)

Bertrand Gröger

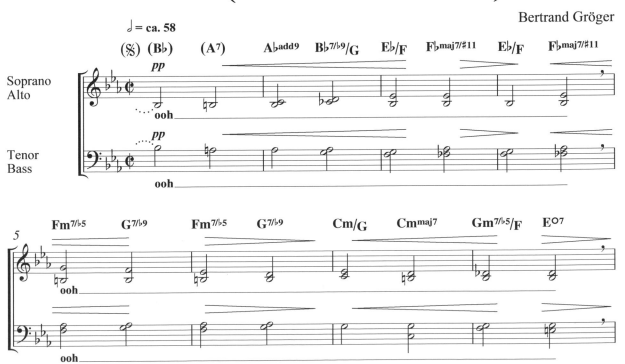

52 813

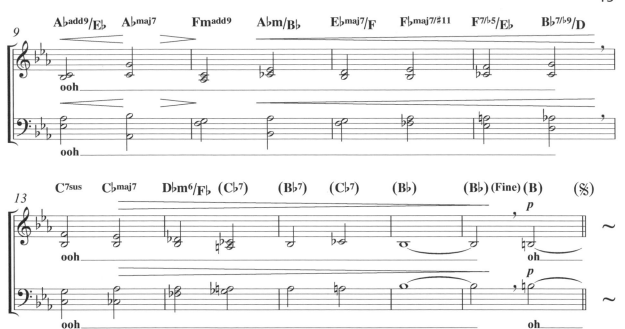

Sing "oh" (as indicated), "aw", "ah" and "ooh" in loops II. - V. while changing expression to *p* (as indicated), *mp*, *mf* and *pp*, respectively.

# Chromatin' Latin

Bertrand Gröger

# Circling in T.

Bertrand Gröger

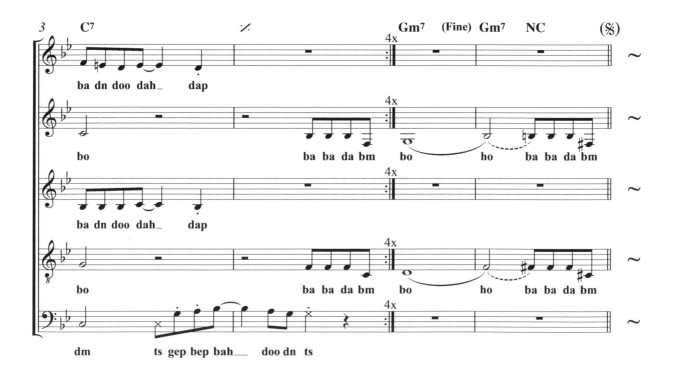

OPTION: **Staggered Beginning** | S2 **(1)** sings first 4 measures alone and is then accompanied by T **(2)**, followed by B **(3)**, S1 **(4)** and A **(5)**.

4-Part: A **(1)** sings first 4 measures alone and is then accompanied by T **(2)**, followed by B **(3)** and S **(4)**.

52 813

# Conversations

Bertrand Gröger

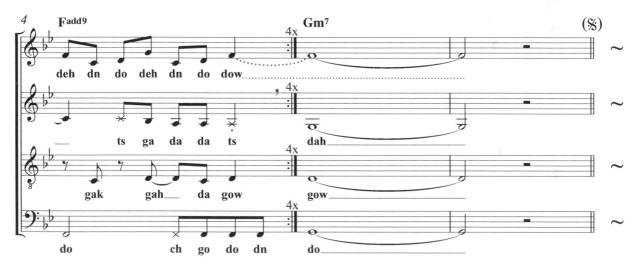

OPTION: **Staggered Beginning** A **(1)** sings first 4 measures alone and is then accompanied by T **(2)**, followed by S **(3)** and B **(4)**.

# Déjà Vu

Bertrand Gröger

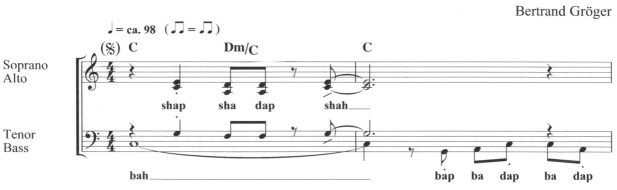

52 813

# Diggeching Samba

Bertrand Gröger

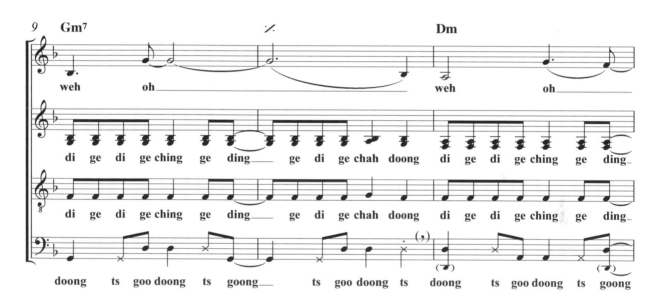

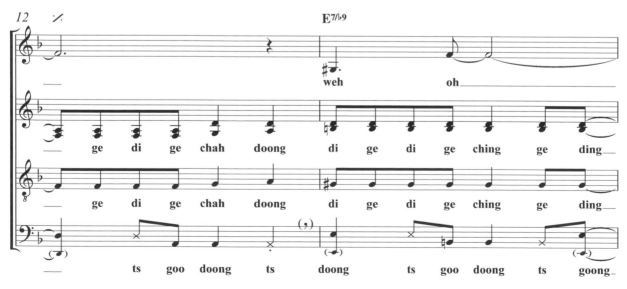

Diggeching Samba    52 813

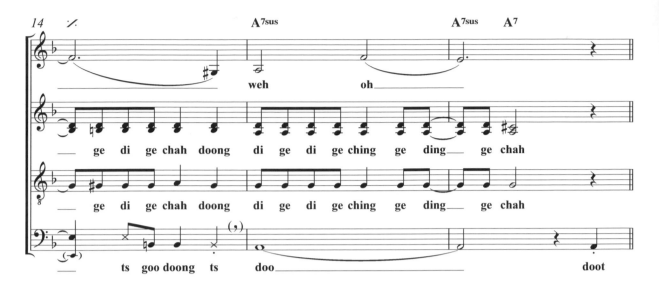

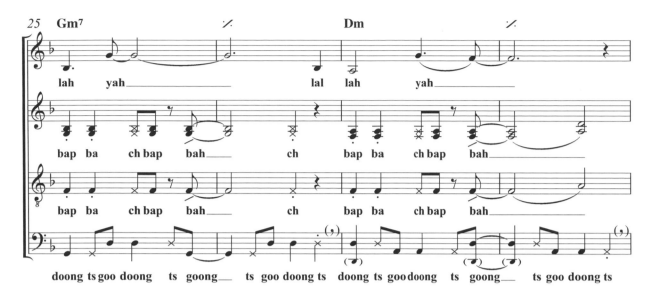

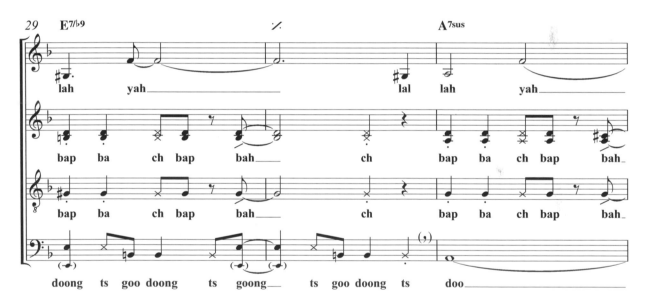

Diggeching Samba
52 813

# Dom-dzom Blues

Bertrand Gröger

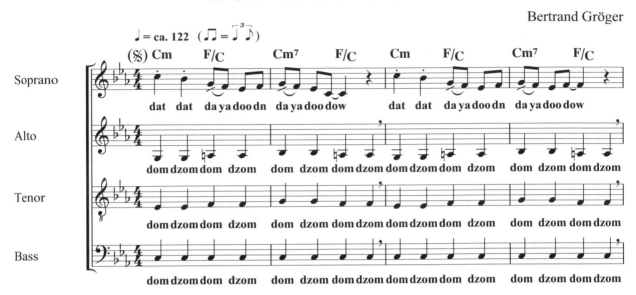

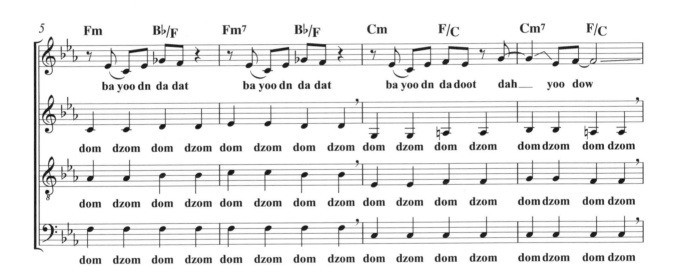

52 813

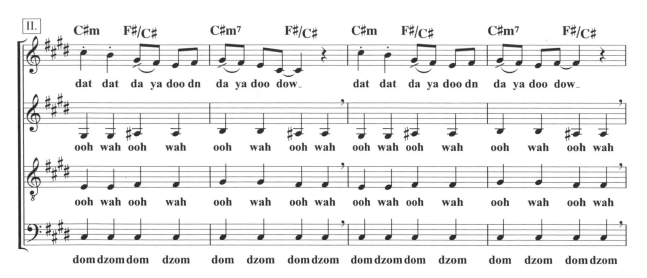

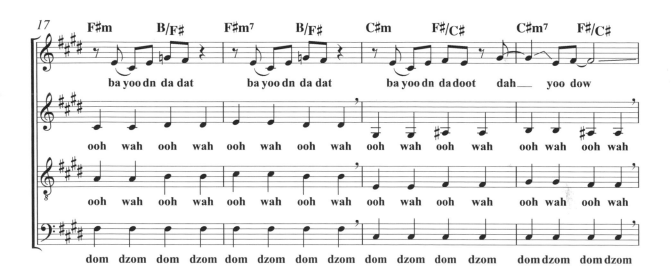

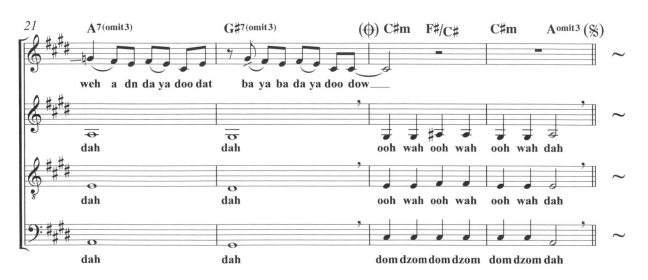

52 813

# Equal Opportunities

Bertrand Gröger

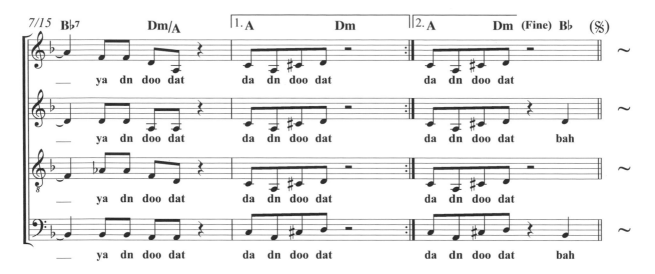

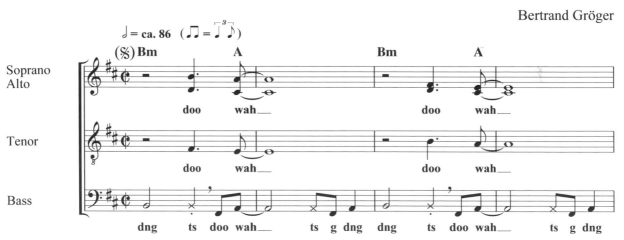

# Face the Bass

Bertrand Gröger

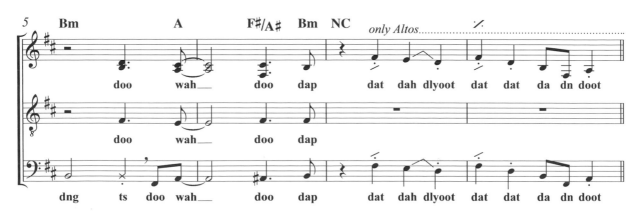

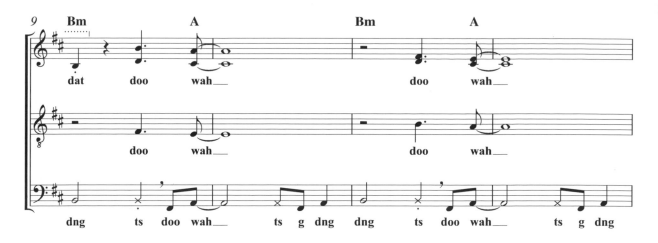

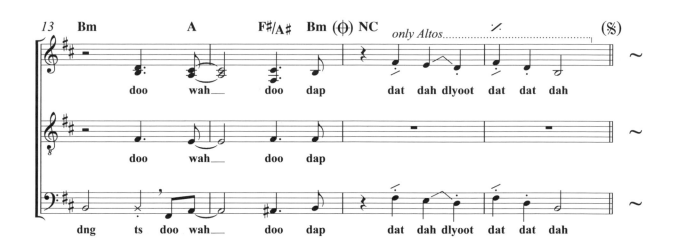

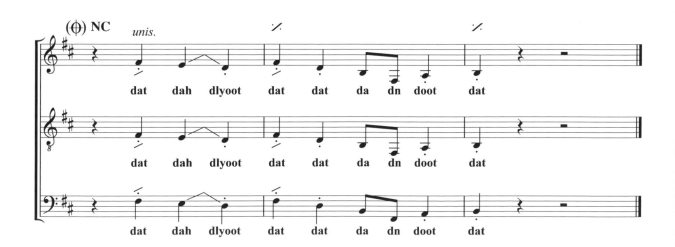

OPTION: Clap Hands or Beat Fist on Chest

# Faster Than Miles

Bertrand Gröger

# Five Fo(u)r the Fifth

Bertrand Gröger

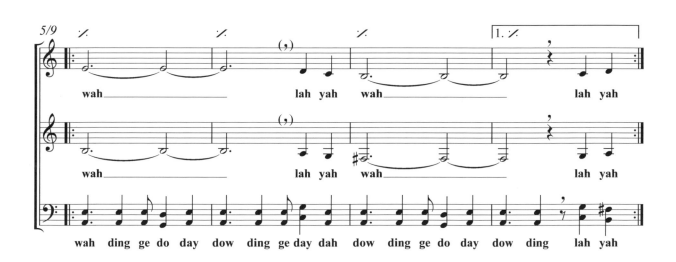

52 813

# Folkus on Three

Bertrand Gröger

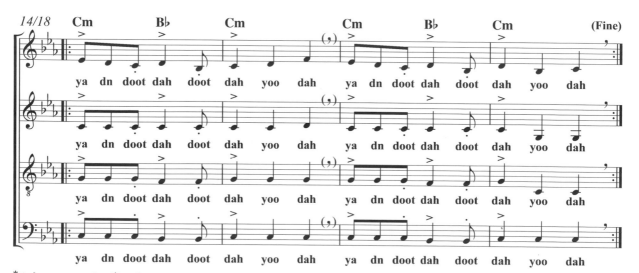

\* to be pronounced as ['hʌŋə]

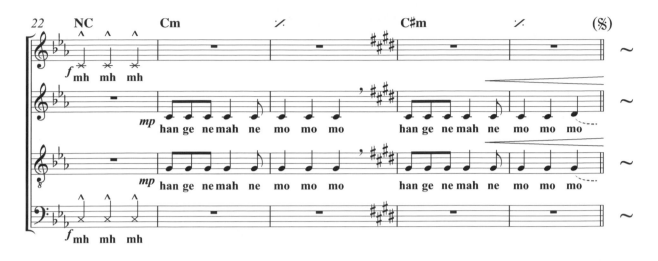

# Gimmix

Bertrand Gröger

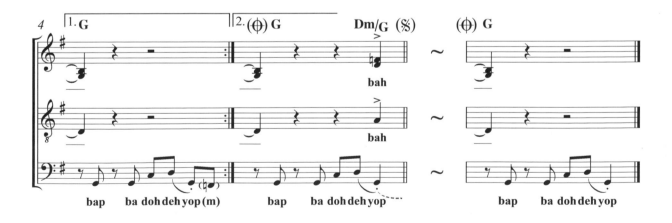

52 813

# Hanging Out

Bertrand Gröger

OPTION: **Tempo Variation** Try other tempi alternatively, e.g. ♩ = 56 / ♩ = 64 / ♩ = 68 / ♩ = 72 / ♩ = 76

# Lah-lah on H-Day

Bertrand Gröger

52 813

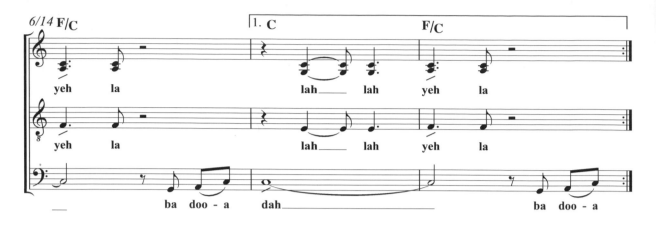

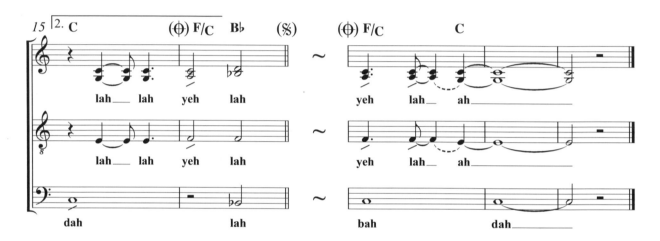

# Lah-yah-nah

Bertrand Gröger

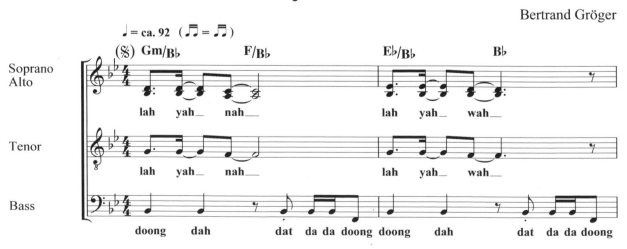

52 813

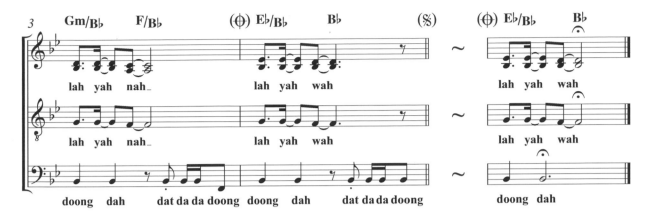

# Latin Bend

Bertrand Gröger

52 813

# Let's Doo It

Bertrand Gröger

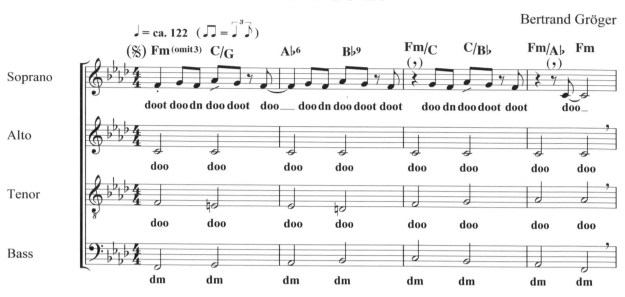

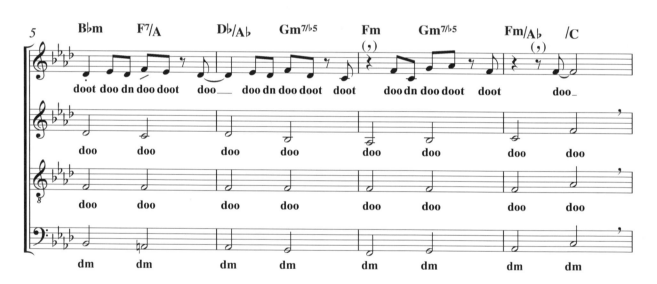

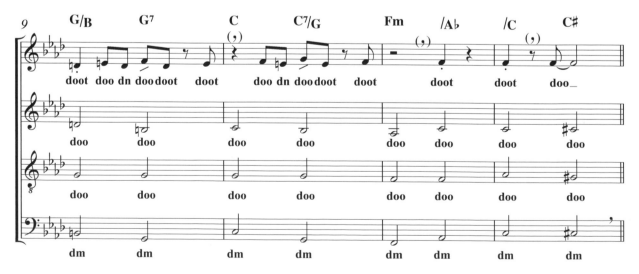

52 813

Fade out on cue in loop IX.

OPTION: Finger Snaps

# Locomotion

Bertrand Gröger

Fade out on cue in loop IX.

OPTION: Finger Snaps

# Major Swing

Bertrand Gröger

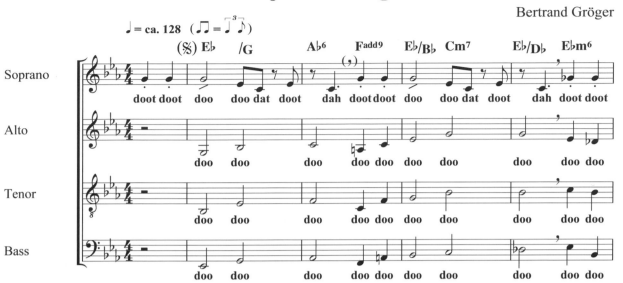

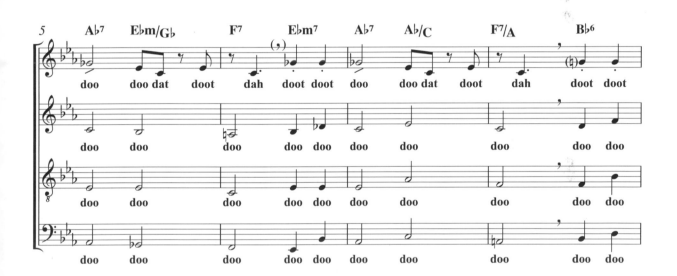

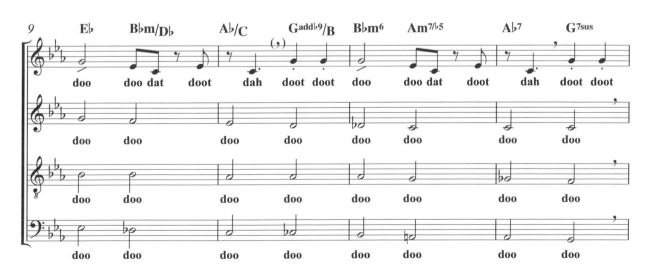

36

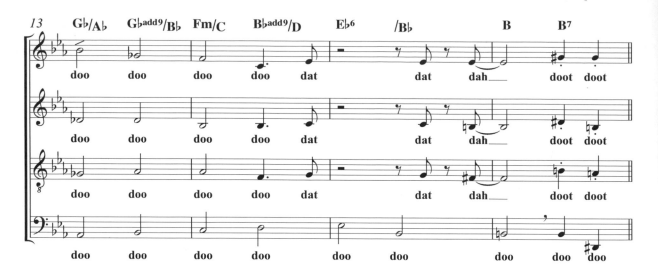

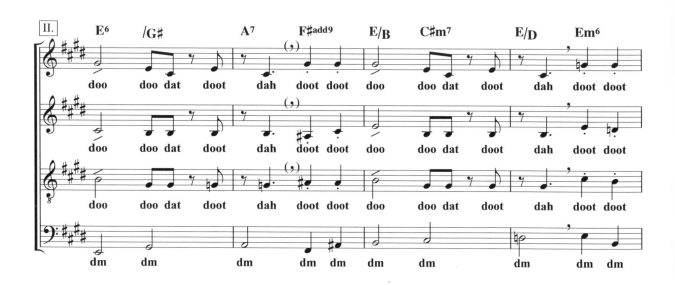

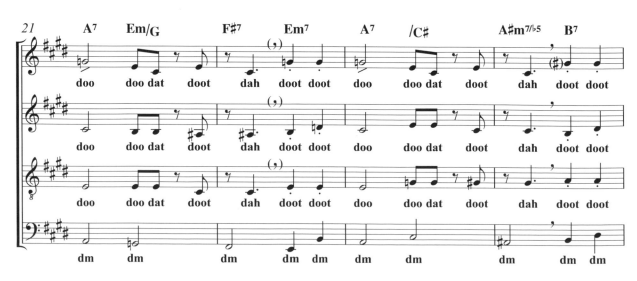

Major Swing                    52 813                    D O  N O T  C O P Y

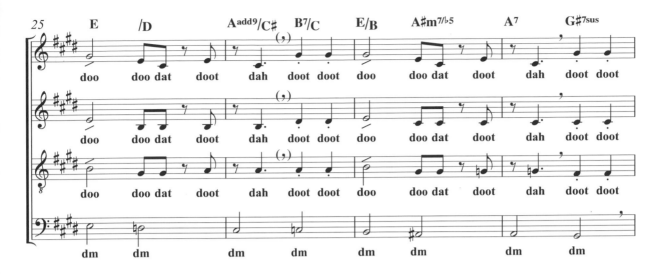

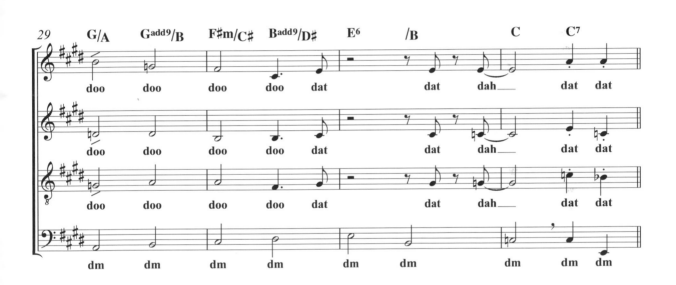

52 813

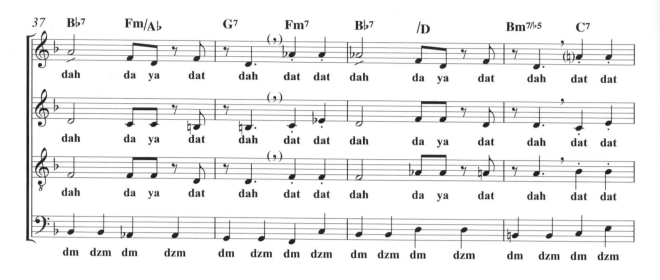

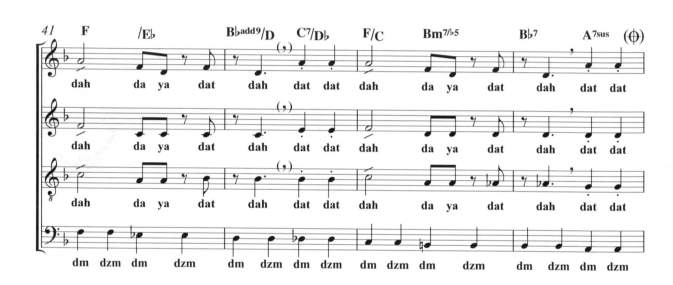

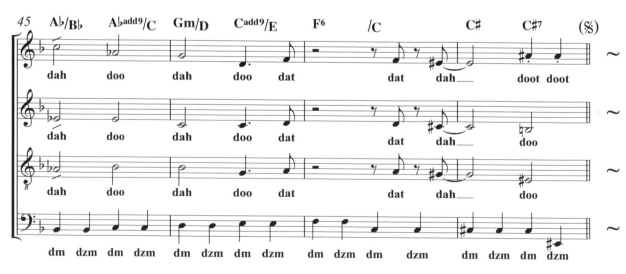

52 813

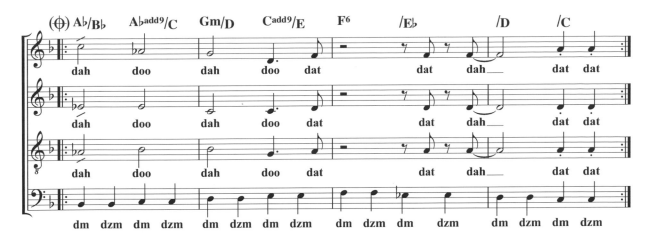

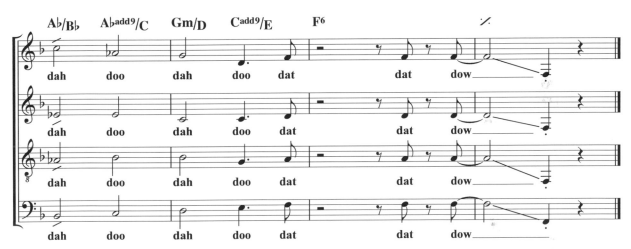

# Oh-weh

Bertrand Gröger

52 813

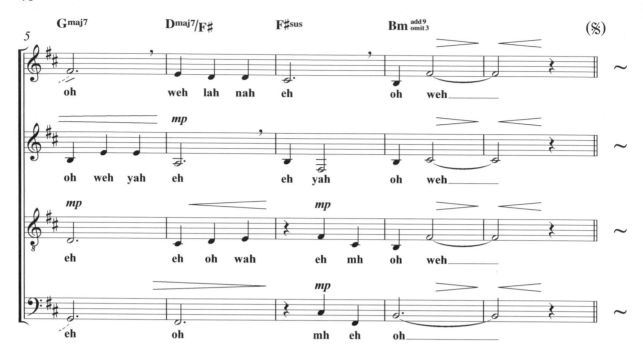

# Open Space

Bertrand Gröger

# Perfect Day

Bertrand Gröger

# Plenty of Twenty

Bertrand Gröger

# Restless Minority

Bertrand Gröger

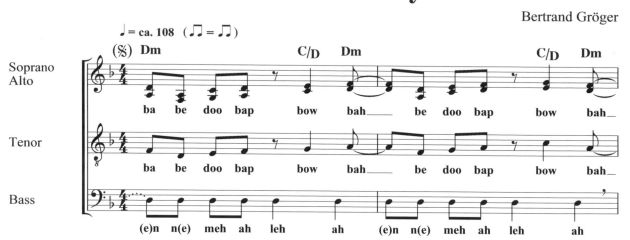

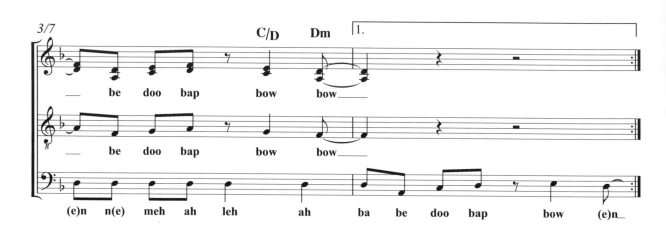

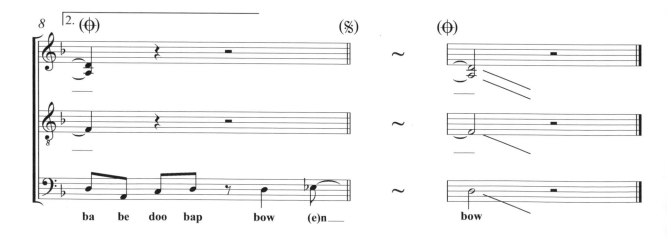

# Revel in African Seven

Bertrand Gröger

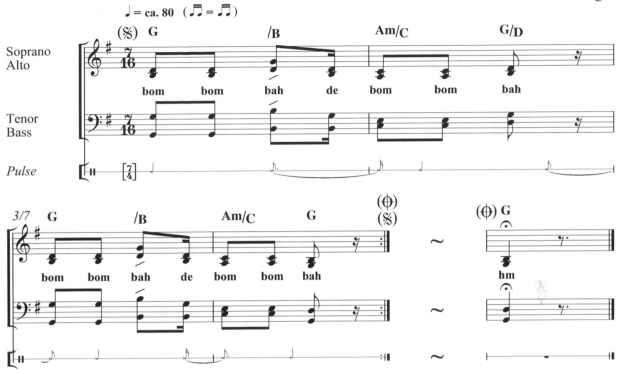

OPTION (a): **Feel the pulse...** | Clap your hands, stomp your feet, beat your chest, or slap your thighs following the steady quarters pulse

OPTION (b): **...and backbeat** | Add backbeat hand claps or finger snaps to above

# Rocket Joe

Bertrand Gröger

52 813

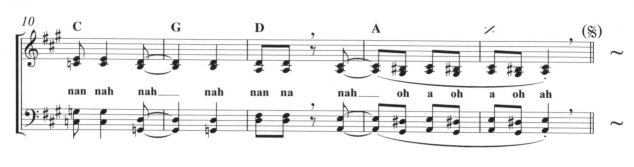

| OPTION (a): Lyrics Variation | Instead of "nah" sing: "hoo" / "lee" / "mo" / "dvv" (imitating the sound of a distorted guitar) |

| OPTION (b): Hand Claps | (preferably when singing "nah") |

# Saturday Groove

Bertrand Gröger

52 813

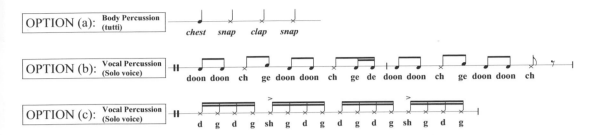

# Seven to the Blues

Bertrand Gröger

48

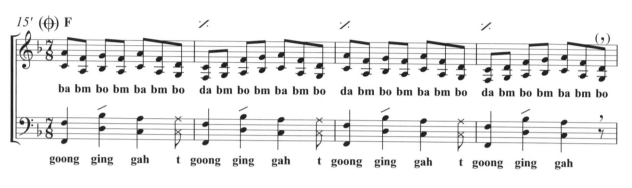

Seven to the Blues

52 813

D O   N O T   C O P Y

# Shaken, Not Stirred

Bertrand Gröger

52 813

OPTION: Finger Snaps

# Shut Up

Bertrand Gröger

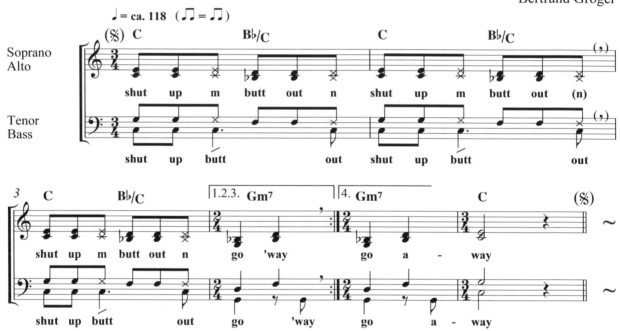

# Straight Ahead

Bertrand Gröger

52 813

52 813

# Strolling

Bertrand Gröger

52 813

# Swingin' Easy

Bertrand Gröger

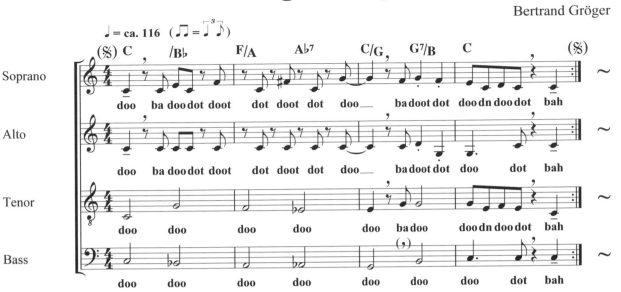

# Take It Off

Bertrand Gröger

52 813

OPTION (a): **Soprano I or Solo Voice**

deh ya bm do ba deh bm beh bo dehp bohp bow ya ba dehp bow

ya ba dehp bow beh yow wa bm dohp bow wa bm dohp bow

OPTION (b): **Instead of (a) improvise on**

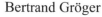

OPTION (c): **Vocal Percussion (Solo voice)**

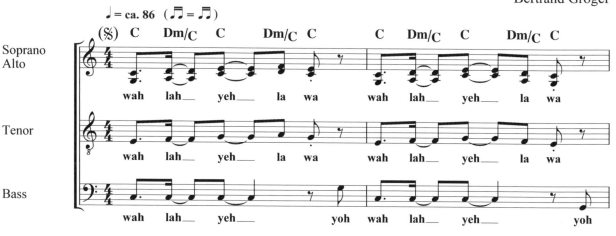

doong k t k ch k t goong k t k ch k t k doong k t k ch k t k doong mh

# Wah-lah-yeh

Bertrand Gröger

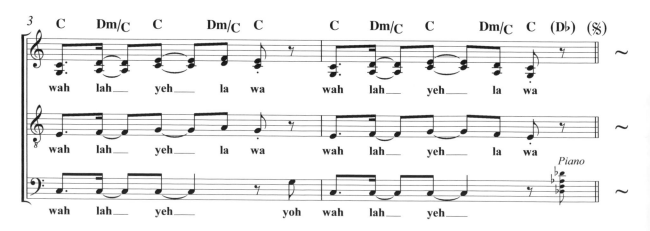

Soprano Alto

wah lah___ yeh___ la wa wah lah___ yeh___ la wa

Tenor

wah lah___ yeh___ la wa wah lah___ yeh___ la wa

Bass

wah lah___ yeh___ yoh wah lah___ yeh___ yoh

wah lah___ yeh___ la wa wah lah___ yeh___ la wa

wah lah___ yeh___ la wa wah lah___ yeh___ la wa

wah lah___ yeh___ yoh wah lah___ yeh___

*Piano*

OPTION: **Hand Claps**

Schott Music, Mainz 52 813